Henry Wadsworth
LONGFELLOW
Selected Poems

Edited and with an Introduction
by C. Merton Babcock
Illustrations by Wendy Watson

———

PETER PAUPER PRESS, INC.
White Plains • New York

FOREWORD

*Henry Wadsworth Longfellow (1807-1882),
the most popular of American poets, was
able to capture the minds and hearts of his
readers by the steadfast sincerity of his con-
victions and the disarming simplicity of his
verses. His own "impassioned experiences"
equipped him with an enviable power for
turning men from the burdens of their earth-
ly cares to a contemplation of the highest
transcendent truths. As poet of the hearth
and home, of the mysteries and enigmas of
human experience, of natural beauty, of the
sea, of death, and of the soul, he endeared
himself to lovers of poetry around the world.
As defender of such American ideals and as-
pirations as optimism, perfectibility, passion
for truth, devotion to God, and love of coun-
try, he became distinguished as "the national
bard." Because of the earnestness and dig-
nity and grace which Longfellow brought to
his art, the verses have been inscribed on the
memories of all Americans, and have become
a veritable folklore of treasured sentiments
and respected traditions. For sheer beauty,*

*few poems in the English language rival the
sustained harmonies and rhapsodies of many
of Longfellow's lyrics. As we read them, "the
tumult of the time disconsolate to inarticu-
late murmurs dies away."*

*Space limitations forbid the inclusion in this
volume of the long narrative poems for
which the author is so well remembered.
Many readers will want to avail themselves
of the complete works in order to discover
that inward serenity which is Longfellow's
unmistakable signature.*

THE EDITOR

SELECTED POEMS
OF
HENRY WADSWORTH
LONGFELLOW

Selected Poems

THE CHILDREN'S HOUR

Between the dark and the daylight,
   When the night is beginning to lower,
Comes a pause in the day's occupation,
   That is known as the Children's Hour.

I hear in the chamber above me
   The patter of little feet,
The sound of a door that is opened,
   And voices soft and sweet.

From my study I see in the lamplight,
   Descending the broad hall stair,
Grave Alice, and laughing Allegra,
   And Edith with golden hair.

A whisper, and then a silence:
   Yet I know by their merry eyes

They are plotting and planning together
    To take me by surprise.

A sudden rush from the stairway,
    A sudden raid from the hall!
By three doors left unguarded
    They enter my castle wall!

They climb up into my turret
    O'er the arms and back of my chair;
If I try to escape, they surround me;
    They seem to be everywhere.

They almost devour me with kisses,
    Their arms about me entwine,
Till I think of the Bishop of Bingen
    In his Mouse-Tower on the Rhine!

Do you think, O blue-eyed banditti,
    Because you have scaled the wall,
Such an old mustache as I am
    Is not a match for you all!

I have you fast in my fortress,
    And will not let you depart,

8

But put you down into the dungeon
    In the round-tower of my heart.

And there will I keep you forever.
    Yes, forever and a day,
Till the walls shall crumble to ruin,
    And moulder in dust away!

THE SOUND OF THE SEA

The sea awoke at midnight from its sleep,
    And round the pebbly beaches far and
        wide
    I heard the first wave of the rising tide
    Rush onward with uninterrupted sweep;
A voice out of the silence of the deep,
    A sound mysteriously multiplied
    As of a cataract from the mountain's side,
    Or roar of winds upon a wooded steep.
So comes to us at times, from the unknown
    And inaccessible solitudes of being,
    The rushing of the sea-tides of the soul;
And inspirations, that we deem our own,
    Are some divine foreshadowing and
        foreseeing
    Of things beyond our reason or control.

PAUL REVERE'S RIDE

Listen, my children, and you shall hear
Of the midnight ride of Paul Revere,
On the eighteenth of April, in Seventy-five;
Hardly a man is now alive
Who remembers that famous day and year.

He said to his friend, "If the British march
By land or sea from the town to-night,
Hang a lantern aloft in the belfry arch
Of the North Church tower as a signal
    light, —
One, if by land, and two, if by sea;
And I on the opposite shore will be,
Ready to ride and spread the alarm
Through every Middlesex village and farm,
For the country folk to be up and to arm."

Then he said, "Good-night!" and with
    muffled oar
Silently rowed to the Charlestown shore,
Just as the moon rose over the bay,
Where swinging wide at her moorings lay
The Somerset, British man-of-war;
A phantom ship, with each mast and spar

Across the moon like a prison bar,
And a huge black-hulk, that was magnified
By its own reflection in the tide.

Meanwhile, his friend, through alley and
  street,
Wanders and watches with eager ears,
Till in the silence around him he hears
The muster of men at the barrack door,
The sound of arms, and the tramp of feet,
And the measured tread of the grenadiers,
Marching down to their boats on the shore.

Then he climbed the tower of the Old North
  Church,
By the wooden stairs, with stealthy tread,
To the belfry-chamber overhead,
And startled the pigeons from their perch
On the sombre rafters, that round him made
Masses and moving shapes of shade, —
By the trembling ladder, steep and tall,
To the highest window in the wall,
Where he paused to listen and look down
A moment on the roofs of the town,
And the moonlight flowing over all.

Beneath, in the churchyard, lay the dead,
In their night-encampment on the hill,
Wrapped in silence so deep and still
That he could hear, like a sentinel's tread,
The watchful night-wind, as it went
Creeping along from tent to tent,
And seeming to whisper, "All is well!"
A moment only he feels the spell
Of the place and the hour, and the secret
    dread
Of the lonely belfry and the dead;
For suddenly all his thoughts are bent
On a shadowy something far away,
Where the river widens to meet the bay, —
A line of black that bends and floats
On the rising tide, like a bridge of boats.

Meanwhile, impatient to mount and ride,
Booted and spurred, with a heavy stride
On the opposite shore walked Paul Revere.
Now he patted his horse's side,
Now gazed at the landscape far and near,
Then, impetuous, stamped the earth,
And turned and tightened his saddle-girth;
But mostly he watched with eager search

The belfry-tower of the Old North Church,
As it rose above the graves on the hill,
Lonely and spectral and sombre and still.
And lo! as he looks, on the belfry's height
A glimmer, and then a gleam of light!
He springs to the saddle, the bridle he turns,
But lingers and gazes, till full on his sight
A second lamp in the belfry burns!

A hurry of hoofs in a village street,
A shape in the moonlight, a bulk in the dark,
And beneath, from the pebbles, in passing,
   a spark
Struck out by a steed flying fearless and fleet:
That was all! And yet, through the gloom
   and the light,
The fate of a nation was riding that night;
And the spark struck out by that steed, in
   his flight,
Kindled the land into flame with its heat.
He has left the village and mounted the
   steep,
And beneath him, tranquil and broad and
   deep,
Is the Mystic, meeting the ocean tides;

And under the alders, that skirt its edge,
Now soft on the sand, now loud on the ledge,
Is heard the tramp of his steed as he rides.

It was twelve by the village clock,
When he crossed the bridge into Medford
    town.
He heard the crowing of the cock,
And the barking of the farmer's dog,
And felt the damp of the river fog,
That rises after the sun goes down.

It was one by the village clock,
When he galloped into Lexington.
He saw the gilded weathercock
Swim in the moonlight as he passed,
And the meeting-house windows, blank
    and bare,
Gaze at him with a spectral glare,
As if they already stood aghast
At the bloody work they would look upon.

It was two by the village clock,
When he came to the bridge in Concord
    town.

He heard the bleating of the flock,
And the twitter of birds among the trees,
And felt the breath of the morning breeze
Blowing over the meadows brown.
And one was safe and asleep in his bed
Who at the bridge would be first to fall,
Who that day would be lying dead,
Pierced by a British musket-ball.

You know the rest. In the books you have
    read,
How the British Regulars fired and fled, —
How the farmers gave them ball for ball,
From behind each fence and farm-yard wall,
Chasing the red-coats down the lane,
Then crossing the fields to emerge again
Under the trees at the turn of the road,
And only pausing to fire and load.

So through the night rode Paul Revere;
And so through the night went his cry of
    alarm
To every Middlesex village and farm, —
A cry of defiance and not of fear,
A voice in the darkness, a knock at the door,

And a word that shall echo forevermore!
For, borne on the night-wind of the Past,
Through all our history, to the last,
In the hour of darkness and peril and need,
The people will waken and listen to hear
The hurrying hoof-beats of that steed,
And the midnight message of Paul Revere.

THE VILLAGE BLACKSMITH

Under a spreading chestnut-tree
    The village smithy stands;
The smith, a mighty man is he,
    With large and sinewy hands;
And the muscles of his brawny arms
    Are strong as iron bands.

His hair is crisp, and black, and long,
    His face is like the tan;
His brow is wet with honest sweat,
    He earns whate'er he can,
And looks the whole world in the face,
    For he owes not any man.

Week in, week out, from morn till night,
    You can hear his bellows blow;

You can hear him swing his heavy sledge,
  With measured beat and slow,
Like a sexton ringing the village bell,
  When the evening sun is low.

And children coming home from school
  Look in at the open door;
They love to see the flaming forge,
  And hear the bellows roar,
And catch the burning sparks that fly
  Like chaff from a threshing-floor.

He goes on Sunday to the church,
  And sits among his boys;
He hears the parson pray and preach,
  He hears his daughter's voice,
Singing in the village choir,
  And it makes his heart rejoice.

It sounds to him like her mother's voice,
  Singing in Paradise!
He needs must think of her once more,
  How in the grave she lies;
And with his hard, rough hand he wipes
  A tear out of his eyes.

Toiling, — rejoicing, — sorrowing,
    Onward through life he goes;
Each morning sees some task begin,
    Each evening sees it close;
Something attempted, something done,
    Has earned a night's repose.

Thanks, thanks to thee, my worthy friend,
    For the lesson thou hast taught!
Thus at the flaming forge of life
    Our fortunes must be wrought;
Thus on its sounding anvil shaped
Each burning deed and thought.

THE DAY IS DONE

The day is done, and the darkness
    Falls from the wings of Night,
As a feather is wafted downward
    From an eagle in his flight.

I see the lights of the village
    Gleam through the rain and the mist,
And a feeling of sadness comes o'er me
    That my soul cannot resist:

A feeling of sadness and longing,
    That is not akin to pain,
And resembles sorrow only
    As the mist resembles the rain.

Come, read to me some poem,
    Some simple and heartfelt lay,
That shall soothe this restless feeling,
    And banish the thoughts of day.

Not from the grand old masters,
    Not from the bards sublime,
Whose distant footsteps echo
    Through the corridors of Time.

For, like strains of martial music,
    Their mighty thoughts suggest
Life's endless toil and endeavor;
    And tonight I long for rest.

Read from some humbler poet,
    Whose songs gushed from his heart,
As showers from the clouds of summer,
    Or tears from the eyelids start;

Who, through long days of labor,
    And nights devoid of ease,

Still heard in his soul the music
  Of wonderful melodies.

Such songs have power to quiet
  The restless pulse of care,
And come like the benediction
  That follows after prayer.

Then read from the treasured volume
  The poem of thy choice,
And lend to the rhyme of the poet
  The beauty of thy voice.

And the night shall be filled with music,
  And the cares, that infest the day,
Shall fold their tents, like the Arabs,
  And as silently steal away.

HYMN TO THE NIGHT

I heard the trailing garments of the Night
  Sweep through her marble halls!
I saw her sable skirts all fringed with light
  From the celestial walls!
I felt her presence, by its spell of might,

Stoop o'er me from above;
The calm, majestic presence of the Night,
    As of the one I love.

I heard the sounds of sorrow and delight,
    The manifold, soft chimes,
That fill the haunted chambers of the Night,
    Like some old poet's rhymes.

From the cool cisterns of the midnight air
    My spirit drank repose;
The fountain of perpetual peace flows
        there, —
    From those deep cisterns flows.

O holy Night! from thee I learn to bear
    What man has borne before!
Thou layest thy finger on the lips of Care,
    And they complain no more.

Peace! Peace! Orestes-like I breathe this
        prayer!
    Descend with broad-winged flight,
The welcome, the thrice-prayed for, the
        most fair,
    The best-beloved Night!

THE POET AND HIS SONGS

As the birds come in the Spring,
　　We know not from where;
As the stars come at evening
　　From depths of the air;

As the rain comes from the cloud,
　　And the brook from the ground;
As suddenly, low or loud,
　　Out of silence a sound;

As the grape comes to the vine,
　　The fruit to the tree;
As the wind comes to the pine,
　　And the tide to the sea;

As come the white sails of ships
　　O'er the ocean's verge;
As comes the smile to the lips,
　　The foam to the surge;

So come to the Poet his songs,
　　All hitherward blown
From the misty realm, that belongs
　　To the vast Unknown.

His, and not his, are the lays
    He sings; and their fame
Is his, and not his; and the praise
    And the pride of a name.

For voices pursue him by day,
    And haunt him by night,
And he listens, and needs must obey,
    When the Angel says: "Write!"

CATAWBA WINE

    This song of mine
    Is a Song of the Vine,
To be sung by the glowing embers
    Of wayside inns,
    When the rain begins
To darken the drear Novembers.

    It is not a song
    Of the Scuppernong,
From warm Carolinian valleys,
    Nor the Isabel
    And the Muscadel
That bask in our garden alleys.

Nor the red Mustang,
Whose clusters hang
O'er the waves of the Colorado,
And the fiery flood
Of whose purple blood
Has a dash of Spanish Bravado.

For richest and best
Is the wine of the West,
That grows by the Beautiful River;
Whose sweet perfume
Fills all the room
With a benison on the giver.

And as hollow trees
Are the haunts of bees,
Forever going and coming;
So this crystal hive
Is all alive
With a swarming and buzzing and
humming.

Very good in its way
Is the Verzenay,
Or the Sillery soft and creamy;

But Catawba wine
Has a taste more divine,
More dulcet, delicious, and dreamy.

There grows no vine
By the haunted Rhine,
By Danube or Guadalquivir,
Nor on island or cape,
That bears such a grape
As grows by the Beautiful River.

Drugged is their juice
For foreign use,
When shipped o'er the reeling Atlantic,
To rack our brains
With the fever pains.
That have driven the Old World frantic.

To the sewers and sinks
With all such drinks,
And after them tumble the mixer;
For a poison malign
Is such Borgia wine,
Or at best but a devil's Elixir.

While pure as a spring
Is the wine I sing,

And to praise it, one needs but name it;
    For Catawba wine
    Has need of no sign,
No tavern-bush to proclaim it.

    And this Song of the Vine,
    This greeting of mine,
The winds and the birds shall deliver
    To the Queen of the West,
    In her garlands dressed,
On the banks of the Beautiful River.

THE FIRE OF DRIFTWOOD
Devereux Farm, near Marblehead

We sat within the farmhouse old,
    Whose windows, looking o'er the bay,
Gave to the sea breeze damp and cold
    An easy entrance, night and day.

Not far away we saw the port,
    The strange, old-fashioned, silent town,
The lighthouse, the dismantled fort,
    The wooden houses, quaint and brown.

We sat and talked until the night,
    Descending, filled the little room;
Our faces faded from the sight,
    Our voices only broke the gloom.

We spake of many a vanished scene,
    Of what we once had thought and said,
Of what had been, and might have been,
    And who was changed, and who was dead;

And all that fills the hearts of friends,
    When first they feel, with secret pain,
Their lives henceforth have separate ends,
    And never can be one again;

The first slight swerving of the heart,
    That words are powerless to express,
And leave it still unsaid in part,
    Or say it in too great excess.

The very tones in which we spake
    Had something strange, I could but mark;
The leaves of memory seemed to make
    A mournful rustling in the dark.

Oft died the words upon our lips,
　　As suddenly, from out the fire
Built of the wreck of stranded ships,
　　The flames would leap and then expire.

And, as their splendor flashed and failed,
　　We thought of wrecks upon the main,
Of ships dismasted, that were hailed
　　And sent no answer back again.

The windows, rattling in their frames,
　　The ocean, roaring up the beach,
The gusty blast, the bickering flames,
　　All mingled vaguely in our speech;

Until they made themselves a part
　　Of fancies floating through the brain,
The long-lost ventures of the heart,
　　That send no answers back again.

O flames that glowed! O hearts that yearned!
　　They were indeed too much akin,
The driftwood fire without that burned,
　　The thoughts that burned and glowed
　　　　within.

IT IS NOT ALWAYS MAY

The sun is bright, — the air is clear,
  The darting swallows soar and sing,
And from the stately elms I hear
  The bluebird prophesying Spring.

So blue yon winding river flows,
  It seems an outlet from the sky,
Where, waiting till the west-wind blows,
  The freighted clouds at anchor lie.

All things are new; — the buds, the leaves,
  That gild the elm-tree's nodding crest,
And even the nest beneath the eaves; —
  There are no birds in last year's nest!

All things rejoice in youth and love,
  The fullness of their first delight!
And learn from the soft heavens above
  The melting tenderness of night.

Maiden, that read'st this simple rhyme,
  Enjoy thy youth, it will not stay;
Enjoy the fragrance of thy prime,
  For oh, it is not always May!

Enjoy the Spring of Love and Youth,
  To some good angel leave the rest;
For time will teach thee soon the truth,
  There are no birds in last year's nest!

THE CASTLE-BUILDER

A gentle boy, with soft and silken locks,
  A dreamy boy, with brown and tender
    eyes,
A castle-builder, with his wooden blocks,
  And towers that touch imaginary skies.

A fearless rider on his father's knee,
  An eager listener unto stories told
At the Round Table of the nursery,
  Of heroes and adventures manifold.

There will be other towers for thee to
    build;
  There will be other steeds for thee to
    ride;
There will be other legends, and all filled
  With greater marvels and more glorified.

Build on, and make thy castles high and
    fair,
  Rising and reaching upward to the skies;
Listen to voices in the upper air.
  Nor lose thy simple faith in mysteries.

EXCELSIOR

The shades of night were falling fast,
As through an Alpine village passed
A youth, who bore, 'mid snow and ice,
A banner with the strange device,
    Excelsior!

His brow was sad; his eye beneath
Flashed like a falchion from its sheath,
And like a silver clarion rung
The accents of that unknown tongue,
    Excelsior!

In happy homes he saw the light
Of household fires gleam warm and bright;
Above, the spectral glaciers shone,
And from his lips escaped a groan,
    Excelsior!

"Try not the Pass!" the old man said;
"Dark lowers the tempest overhead,
The roaring torrent is deep and wide!"
And loud that clarion voice replied,
　　Excelsior!

"Oh stay," the maiden said, "and rest
Thy weary head upon this breast!"
A tear stood in his bright blue eye,
But still he answered, with a sigh,
　　Excelsior!

"Beware the pine-tree's withered branch!
Beware the awful avalanche!"
This was the peasant's last Good-night,
A voice replied, far up the height,
　　Excelsior!

At break of day, as heavenward
The pious monks of St. Bernard
Uttered the oft-repeated prayer,
A voice cried through the startled air,
　　Excelsior!

A traveller, by the faithful hound,
Half-buried in the snow was found,

Still grasping in his hand of ice
That banner with the strange device,
  Excelsior!

There in the twilight cold and gray,
Lifeless, but beautiful, he lay,
And from the sky, serene and far,
A voice fell, like a falling star,
  Excelsior!

CHRISTMAS BELLS

I heard the bells on Christmas Day
Their old, familiar carols play,
  And wild and sweet
  The words repeat
Of peace on earth, good will to men!

And thought how, as the day had come,
The belfries of all Christendom
  Had rolled along
  The unbroken song
Of peace on earth, good will to men!

Till, ringing, singing on its way,
The world revolved from night to day,
   A voice, a chime,
   A chant sublime
O peace on earth, good will to men!

Then from each black, accursed mouth
The cannon thundered in the South,
   And with the sound
   The carols drowned
Of peace on earth, good will to men!

It was as if an earthquake rent
The hearthstones of a continent,
   And made forlorn
   The households born
Of peace on earth, good will to men!

And in despair I bowed my head;
"There is no peace on earth," I said:
   "For hate is strong,
   And mocks the song
Of peace on earth, good will to men!"

Then pealed the bells more loud and deep:
"God is not dead; nor doth He sleep!

The wrong shall fail,
The Right prevail,
With peace on earth, good will to men!"

MY LOST YOUTH

Often I think of the beautiful town
    That is seated by the sea;
Often in thought go up and down
The pleasant streets of that dear old town,
    And my youth comes back to me.
        And a verse of a Lapland song
        Is haunting my memory still:
"A boy's will is the wind's will,
And the thoughts of youth are long, long
        thoughts."

I can see the shadowy lines of its trees,
    And catch, in sudden gleams,
The sheen of the far-surrounding seas,
And islands that were the Hesperides
    Of all my boyish dreams.
        And the burden of that old song,
        It murmurs and whispers still:

"A boy's will is the wind's will,
And the thoughts of youth are long, long
      thoughts."

I remember the black wharves and the slips,
   And the sea-tides tossing free;
And Spanish sailors with bearded lips,
And the beauty and mystery of the ships,
   And the magic of the sea.
      And the voice of that wayward song
      Is singing and saying still:
"A boy's will is the wind's will,
And the thoughts of youth are long, long
      thoughts."

I remember the bulwarks by the shore,
   And the fort upon the hill;
The sunrise gun, with its hollow roar,
The drum-beat repeated o'er and o'er,
   And the bugle wild and shrill.
      And the music of that old song
      Throbs in my memory still:
"A boy's will is the wind's will,
And the thoughts of youth are long, long
      thoughts."

I remember the sea-fight far away,
　　How it thundered o'er the tide!
And the dead captains, as they lay
In their graves, o'erlooking the tranquil bay,
　　Where they in battle died.
　　　　And the sound of that mournful song
　　　　Goes through me with a thrill:
"A boy's will is the wind's will,
And the thoughts of youth are long, long
　　　　thoughts."

I can see the breezy dome of groves,
　　The shadows of Deering's Woods;
And the friendships old and the early loves
Come back with a Sabbath sound, as of doves
　　In quiet neighborhoods.
　　　　And the verse of that sweet old song,
　　　　It flutters and murmurs still:
"A boy's will is the wind's will,
And the thoughts of youth are long, long
　　　　thoughts."

I remember the gleams and glooms that dart
　　Across the school-boy's brain;
The song and the silence in the heart,

That in part are prophecies, and in part
     Are longings wild and vain.
        And the voice of that fitful song
        Sings on, and is never still:
"A boy's will is the wind's will,
And the thoughts of youth are long, long
           thoughts."

There are things of which I may not speak;
     There are dreams that cannot die;
There are thoughts that make the strong
           heart weak,
And bring a pallor into the cheek,
     And a mist before the eye.
        And the words of that fatal song
        Come over me like a chill:
"A boy's will is the wind's will,
And the thoughts of youth are long, long
           thoughts."

Strange to me now are the forms I meet
     When I visit the dear old town;
But the native air is pure and sweet,
And the trees that o'ershadow each well-
           known street,

As they balance up and down,
   Are singing the beautiful song,
   Are sighing and whispering still:
"A boy's will is the wind's will,
And the thoughts of youth are long, long
      thoughts."

And Deering's Woods are fresh and fair,
   And with joy is almost pain;
My heart goes back to wander there,
And among the dreams of the days that were,
   I find my lost youth again.
      And the strange and beautiful song,
      The groves are repeating it still:
"A boy's will is the wind's will,
And the thoughts of youth are long, long
      thoughts."

THE BUILDING OF THE SHIP

How beautiful she is!
She lies within those arms, that press
Her form with many a soft caress
Of tenderness and watchful care!
Sail forth into the sea, O ship!

Through wind and wave, right onward steer!
The moistened eye, the trembling lip,
Are not the signs of doubt or fear.

Sail forth into the sea of life,
O gentle, loving, trusting wife.
And safe from all adversity
Upon the bosom of that sea
Thy comings and thy goings be!
For gentleness and love and trust
Prevail o'er angry wave and gust;
And in the wreck of noble lives
Something immortal still survives!

Thou, too, sail on, O Ship of State!
Sail on, O Union, strong and great!
Humanity with all its fears,
With all the hopes of future years,
Is hanging breathless on thy fate!
We know what Master laid thy keel.
What Workmen wrought thy ribs of steel,
Who made each mast, and sail, and rope,
What anvils rang, what hammers beat,
In what a forge and what a heat
Were shaped the anchors of thy hope!

Fear not each sudden sound and shock,
'Tis of the wave and not the rock;
'Tis but the flapping of the sail,
And not a rent made by the gale!
In spite of rock and tempest's roar,
In spite of false lights on the shore,
Sail on, nor fear to breast the sea!
Our hearts, our hopes, are all with thee,
Our hearts, our hopes, our prayers, our tears,
Our faith triumphant o'er our fears,
Are all with thee, — are all with thee!

THE BUILDERS

All are architects of Fate,
    Working in these walls of Time;
Some with massive deeds and great
    Some with ornaments of rhyme.

Nothing useless is, or low;
    Each thing in its place is best;
And what seems but idle show
    Strengthens and supports the rest.

For the structure that we raise,
    Time is with materials filled;

Our to-days and yesterdays
    Are the blocks with which we build.

Truly shape and fashion these;
    Leave no yawning gaps between
Think not, because no man sees,
    Such things will remain unseen.

In the elder days of Art,
    Builders wrought with greatest care
Each minute and unseen part;
    For the Gods see everywhere.

Let us do our work as well,
    Both the unseen and the seen;
Make the house, where Gods may dwell
    Beautiful, entire, and clean.

Else our lives are incomplete,
    Standing in these walls of Time,
Broken stairways, where the feet
    Stumble as they seek to climb.

Build to-day, then, strong and sure,
    With a firm and ample base;

And ascending and secure
   Shall to-morrow find its place.

Thus alone can we attain
   To those turrets, where the eye
Sees the world as one vast plain,
   And one boundless reach of sky.

THE ARROW AND THE SONG

I shot an arrow into the air,
It fell to earth, I knew not where;
For, so swiftly it flew, the sight
Could not follow it in its flight.

I breathed a song into the air,
It fell to earth, I knew not where;
For who has sight so keen and strong,
That it can follow the flight of song?

Long, long afterward, in an oak
I found the arrow, still unbroke;
And the song, from beginning to end,
I found again in the heart of a friend.

DIVINA COMMEDIA

Oft have I seen at some cathedral door
   A laborer, pausing in the dust and heat,
   Lay down his burden, and with reverent
      feet
Enter, and cross himself, and on the floor
Kneel to repeat his paternoster o'er;
   Far off the noises of the world retreat;
   The loud vociferations of the street
   Become an undistinguishable roar.
So, as I enter here from day to day,
   And leave my burden at this minster gate,
   Kneeling in prayer, and not ashamed to
      pray,
The tumult of the time disconsolate
   To inarticulate murmurs dies away,
   While the eternal ages watch and wait.

I lift mine eyes, and all the windows blaze
   With forms of saints and holy men who
      died,
   Here martyred and hereafter glorified;
   And the great Rose upon its leaves
      displays

Christ's Triumph, and the angelic
     roundelays,
     With splendor upon splendor multiplied;
     And Beatrice again at Dante's side
     No more rebukes, but smiles her words of
     praise.
And then the organ sounds, and unseen
     choirs
     Sing the old Latin hymns of peace and
     love,
     And benedictions of the Holy Ghost;
And the melodious bells among the spires
     O'er all the house-tops and through
     heaven above
     Proclaim the elevation of the Host!

O star of morning and of liberty!
     O bringer of the light, whose splendor
     shines
     Above the darkness of the Apennines,
     Forerunner of the day that is to be!
The voices of the city and the sea,
     The voices of the mountains and the
     pines,
     Repeat thy song, till the familiar lines

Are footpaths for the thought of Italy!
Thy fame is blown abroad from all the
　　heights,
　　Through all the nations, and a sound is
　　　heard,
　As of a mighty wind, and men devout,
Strangers of Rome, and the new proselytes,
　In their own language hear thy wondrous
　　word,
　And many are amazed and many doubt.

ENDYMION

　The rising moon has hid the stars;
　Her level rays, like golden bars,
　　Lie on the landscape green
　　With shadows brown between.

　And silver white the river gleams,
　As if Diana, in her dreams,
　　Had dropt her silver bow
　　Upon the meadows low.

　On such a tranquil night as this,
　She woke Endymion with a kiss,

When, sleeping in the grove,
He dreamed not of her love.

Like Dian's kiss, unasked, unsought,
Love gives itself, but is not bought;
    Nor voice, nor sound betrays
    Its deep, impassioned gaze.

It comes, — the beautiful, the free,
The crown of all humanity, —
    In silence and alone
    To seek the elected one.

It lifts the boughs, whose shadows deep
Are Life's oblivion, the soul's sleep,
    And kisses the closed eyes
    Of him who slumbering lies.

O weary hearts! O slumbering eyes!
O drooping souls, whose destinies
    Are fraught with fear and pain.
    Ye shall be loved again!

No one is so accursed by fate,
No one so utterly desolate,

But some heart, though unknown,
Responds unto his own.

Responds, — as if with unseen wings,
An angel touched its quivering strings;
    And whispers, in its song,
    "Where hast thou stayed so long?"

THE EVENING STAR

Lo! in the painted oriel of the West,
    Whose panes the sunken sun incarnadines,
    Like a fair lady at her casement, shines
    The evening star, the star of love and rest!
And then anon she doth herself divest
    Of all her radiant garments, and reclines
    Behind the sombre screen of yonder pines,
    With slumber and soft dreams of love
        oppressed.
O my beloved, my sweet Hesperus!
    My morning and my evening star of love!
    My best and gentlest lady! even thus,
As that fair planet in the sky above,
    Dost thou retire unto my rest at night,
    And from thy darkened window fades
        the light.

CURFEW

I

Solemnly, mournfully,
    Dealing its dole,
The curfew bell
    Is beginning to toll.

Cover the embers,
    And put out the light;
Toil comes with the morning,
    And rest with the night.

Dark grow the windows,
    And quenched is the fire;
Sound fades into silence, —
    All footsteps retire.

No voice in the chambers,
    No sound in the hall!
Sleep and oblivion
    Reign over all!

II

The book is completed,
    And closed, like the day;

And the hand that has written it
Lays it away.

Dim grow its fancies;
Forgotten they lie
Like coals in the ashes,
They darken and die.

Song sinks into silence,
The story is told,
The windows are darkened,
The hearthstone is cold.

Darker and darker
The black shadows fall;
Sleep and oblivion
Reign over all.

THE RAINY DAY

The day is cold, and dark, and dreary;
It rains, and the wind is never weary;
The vine still clings to the mouldering wall,
But at every gust the dead leaves fall,
And the day is dark and dreary.

My life is cold, and dark, and dreary;
It rains, and the wind is never weary;
My thoughts still cling to the mouldering
      Past,
But the hopes of youth fall thick in the blast,
  And the days are dark and dreary.

Be still, sad heart! and cease repining;
Behind the clouds is the sun still shining;
Thy fate is the common fate of all,
Into each life some rain must fall,
  Some days must be dark and dreary.

NATURE

As a fond mother, when the day is o'er,
  Leads by the hand her little child to bed,
  Half willing, half reluctant to be led,
  And leave his broken playthings on the
    floor,
Still gazing at them through the open door,
  Nor wholly reassured and comforted
  By promises of others in their stead,
  Which, though more splendid, may not
    please him more;

So Nature deals with us, and takes away
    Our playthings one by one, and by the
        hand
    Leads us to rest so gently, that we go
Scarce knowing if we wish to go or stay,
    Being too full of sleep to understand
    How far the unknown transcends the
        what we know.

THE HARVEST MOON

It is the Harvest Moon! On gilded vanes
    And roofs of villages, on woodland crests
    And their aerial neighborhoods of nests
    Deserted, on the curtained window-panes
Of rooms where children sleep, on country
        lanes
    And harvest-fields, its mystic splendor
        rests!
    Gone are the birds that were our summer
        guests;
    With the last sheaves return the laboring
        wains!
All things are symbols: the external shows
    Of Nature have their image in the mind,

As flowers and fruits and falling of the
    leaves;
The song-birds leave us at the summer's
    close,
    Only the empty nests are left behind,
    And pipings of the quail among the
        sheaves.

A PSALM OF LIFE

Tell me not, in mournful numbers,
    Life is but an empty dream! —
For the soul is dead that slumbers,
    And things are not what they seem.

Life is real! Life is earnest!
    And the grave is not its goal;
Dust thou art, to dust returnest,
Was not spoken of the soul.

Not enjoyment, and not sorrow,
    Is our destined end or way;
But to act, that each to-morrow
    Find us farther than to-day.

Art is long, and Time is fleeting,
    And our hearts, though stout and brave,

Still like muffled drums, are beating
    Funeral marches to the grave.

In the world's broad field of battle,
    In the bivouac of Life,
Be not like dumb, driven cattle!
    Be a hero in the strife!

Trust no Future, howe'er pleasant!
    Let the dead Past bury its dead!
Act, — act in the living Present!
    Heart within, and God o'erhead!

Lives of great men all remind us
    We can make our lives sublime,
And, departing, leave behind us
    Footprints on the sands of time;

Footprints, that perhaps another,
    Sailing o'er life's solemn main,
A forlorn and shipwrecked brother,
Seeing, shall take heart again.

Let us, then, be up and doing,
    With a heart for any fate;
Still achieving, still pursuing,
    Learn to labor and to wait.